# Let Me Open
You a Swan

Cover art: Dissection of the Thorax of a Cadaver, by Guy de Pavia
Musée Condé, Chantilly, France

Author photo by Fidel Mejia

Book design by Joel A. Bass

ISBN: 978-1-932418-36-1

Elixir Press
PO Box 27029
Denver, Colorado 80227

www.ElixirPress.com

Elixir Press is a nonprofit literary organization.



Library of Congress Cataloging-in-Publication Data


Bogen, Deborah, 1950-
Let me open you a swan : poems / by Deborah Bogen.
p. cm.
ISBN 978-1-932418-36-1 (alk. paper)
I. Title.


PS3602.O425L47 2010
811.6—dc22
2009031604

# Let Me Open
# You a Swan

## Deborah Bogen

# Acknowledgements

Grateful thanks to the editors of the following journals in which these poems (sometimes under different titles and in slightly different versions) originally appeared:

Crazyhorse; *Ghost Images, Using a Blue Willow Pattern, the Anesthesiologist Explains the Procedure, Asylum*

The Gettysburg Review; *Six in the Second Place, Six at the Beginning, Six in the Fifth Place, Six at the Beginning Again, Charity*

Green Mountains Review; *Transubstantiation*

The Iowa Review; *Cantilevered Bedtime Story*

La Fovea; *The Lesson I Taught Myself, Working to Decipher the Body*

MARGIE/The American Journal of Poetry; *Dakota Grandmother Teachings*

New Letters; *Angels*

Plainspoke; *Special Ed Girl, Dakota Schism, Dakota Omphalos*

Ploughshares; *The Rudest Gesture is the Phone that Rings in the Night*

Poemeleon; *The Artist's Statement , Young Swan, Injured Swan, About a Girl I once Was*

Sentence; *Vocabulary Lesson*

Superstition Review; *Pre-Destinaton, The Migraine's Art, Suicide, For My Reader: a Long-Dead Sister*

In addition: Poetry Daily featured *Six at the Beginning* and *Six at the Beginning Again* on their website and included *Six at the Beginning* in their 2007 print anthology, *Poetry Daily Essentials*. Verse Daily featured *Cantilevered Bedtime Story*, and *Special Ed Girl* on their website. *Cantilevered Bedtime Story* was also featured on The Daily Palette website. *Angels* (under the title *The Doctrine of Angels*) was featured on the New Letters website.

Heartfelt thanks to the Monday Night Writing Group and to New York poet Scott Hightower, for steadfast literary companionship. Eternal thanks to my talented and many-faceted husband, Jim Bogen, whose capacity for encouragement and love makes extraordinary things possible. I am indebted to Lynn Emanuel whose poetic example and perceptively inventive reading of many of these poems pushed me to new places. Thank you to Dana Curtis and Elixir Press for putting poetry in print and to you, whoever you are, holding this book in your hands. Let us go on writing and reading each other.

## Dedication

This book is for two amazing women, Wendy King and Robin Mejia. Thank you, my dears, for waking me up.

It is also dedicated to Vera Boots Esperseth who taught me that loyalty is the bedrock of love and to the memory of David Bogen whose generosity changed my life.

# Table of Contents

Autopsy ...................................................................1

LANDSCAPE

Ghost Images................................................5
Asylum ............................................................6
Using a Blue Willow Pattern the Anesthesiologist
    Explains the Procedure................................ 11
Study Guide ................................................. 12
Dakota Schism............................................. 13
Pre-Destination............................................ 14
Cantilevered Bedtime Story....................... 15
Dakota Grandmother Teachings ............... 16
Six in the Second Place ............................... 17
Dakota Omphalos ....................................... 18
Suicide............................................................ 19
Special Ed Girl.............................................. 20
Dakota Migraine.......................................... 21

RELIGION

Sin.................................................................... 25
Angels............................................................. 26
Death House Cleared of Belongings ......... 27
Vocabulary Lesson....................................... 28
How at an Early Age I Became Interested in the Mysteries.. 29
Charity ........................................................... 30
The Book of Changes ................................... 31
The Rudest Gesture is the Phone that Rings in the Night.. 32
This White Bird is Not the Swan ............... 33
The Lesson I Taught Myself........................ 34
Poem For My Reader: A Long-dead Sister ........................... 35

Transubstantiation ....................................................... 36

Placebo Singers ............................................................ 37

Sunday, Resurrecting Berrigan ................................... 38

Six at the Beginning Again ......................................... 39

Question ...................................................................... 40

Resurrection ............................................................... 41

MIGRAINE

Dear My Muse .............................................................. 45

Six at the Beginning.................................................... 46

Grief is My Addiction ................................................. 47

for Pedigree, see Bloodline ........................................ 48

Purgatory .................................................................... 50

Migraine With Aura .................................................... 51

Discipline..................................................................... 52

Migraine Without Aura ............................................... 53

Threshold..................................................................... 54

What Thomas McGrath Taught Me ........................... 55

ART

Dream Poem ................................................................ 59

About a Girl I Once Was............................................. 60

Working to Decipher the Body................................... 61

Young Swan.................................................................. 62

Dear Berrigan, You Died............................................. 63

The Migraine's Art ...................................................... 64

Concerning Failure ..................................................... 65

Injured Swan ............................................................... 66

The Artist's Statement................................................. 67

Words I Had to Teach My Spellcheck ........................ 68

The Human Condition ................................................ 69

Forgiveness Poem........................................................ 70

Fire, and the Sewing of Sky ........................................ 71

To See for Yourself ...................................................... 72

# Introduction

According to swan lore, the constellation Cygnus (or Swan) was called the Northern Cross, which symbolized in antiquity the Cross of Calvary. The Roman Emperor Constantine, according to legend, saw the conjunction of the planets Saturn, Jupiter, Mars, and Venus at the time when he began the process of establishing Christianity as the official religion of his Empire. In other words, he saw the Swan in the stars, when it was high in the sky, and said *"In hoc signe vinces,"* "by this sign you will conquer." With this saying, he might have been making a pun doubling on *"In hoc cygno vinces,"* or "By this swan you will conquer."

Deborah Bogen calls this newest book *Let Me Open You a Swan*, and with this title suggests she will nourish the reader or she will sacrifice something sacred for the reader. If she sacrifices a swan, she will also be giving the reader its last song, an ephemeral relic of astonishing beauty.

I have never heard a swan's last song, but I have heard the swans that swam up to my boat in Lough Glenveagh in Ireland, begging for food, and I can say with certainty that healthy swans nowhere near dying absolutely roar, an ironic and startling sound. This is why I think Bogen's title works marvelously. She gives us the roar and the song at once…because Bogen's speaker in these poems sees the beauty in pain, and therefore distrusts beauty even as she acknowledges its pull, its *hold*, as in "Ghost Images":

> And within the camera [opening : closing] fireworks.
> I mean within the empty box the light's frantic,
> grappling with: *the monk, the match, the gasoline.*

The mind is likewise occupied, its light piteously stark, distorted
—but which of us can ever look away?

One might be tempted to say that her poems infer cures for pain, yet the poems are not about illness; they are about life, and life is not an illness. Bogen writes in the book's inaugural poem, "And you are also here, witness/to these rituals, the aligning of descendant with/descendant, cause with cause" (Autopsy: To See For Yourself"). Likewise, the poems are about the pains in childhood, but childhood is not an illness. And Illness is a matter of perspective, Bogen says in "Special Ed Girl":

> But her thoughts were a slow migration,
>           this way, they said, feel this.
> And she had come to love her own words.
>           *Brickle.*    *Astromi.*    *Desirening.*
>
> It's unreasonable, they told her, loving what explains
> nothing—
> but the words lodged themselves in her chest between
>
> the *slickery* heart and the *milkrinous* spine.

And although Bogen's poems are not poems of grief, perhaps this *opening of a swan* should help us live with pain that is not a symptom of biological illness but of injury, pain that is heartbreak, pain that is grief, and poultice that is the action of getting on with it—life, a normal walk next to peril, which we find in "The Book of Changes, Berrigan":

> ...At the library, bums still
> huddle on the structured steps, turning in this light to stones.
> Confucious flew on Ten Wings, Ted, still no one knows a
> teaching for *I miss you*. In the shade of the dinosaur my
> babies parade waving their innocent flags.

If we take Constantine's experience to heart, he looked to the swan for strength; he did not open the swan. Of course, that story was so long ago. Bogen's poems demand the gesture of generosity, of sacrifice (the opening of a swan). Whereas, Constantine's serene proclamation foreshadows a massacre ("*In hoc signe vinces*"), Bogen inaugurates with an act of violence that invites a kind of residual peace, as in "To See For Yourself":

> You'll need a bone saw and a skull chisel,
> a scalpel and scissors. You'll need
> toothed forceps, a basin of water—...

It's love that knuckles down, that struggles
to tell the tumor from the bright idea,
paring memory to bone and turning truth to
something better than monument.
There will be months and years when you can't
see, a gauzy past in the air and no light.
Then one day, the flock lifts.

The flock… *Landscape, Religion, Migraine, Art*… these are the section titles of *Let Me Open You a Swan*, and these may very well be the issues that shape this poet's work. They are also the issues that shape the poet's voice, and hone her impeccable craft. All are bound up by the image, so that the poet's line may be governed by the visual sprawl of each. What this means in Bogen's book is that the poems almost never resemble one another on the page, from one poem to the next. The book *moves* and *breathes* because of this.

But what really kept me reading my first time through the book was the language, the breath-taking sounds of alliterative verse, the beautiful and the rough-and-tumble of a buggy ride through the country in "Asylum":

On a flatbed where they stacked the bales
I stood singing, or

I sat on a splintered bench in Sunday School humming or

I followed Old John to the mouth of the Missouri where
he yanked slick fishes out.

Deborah Bogen is the real thing, and she knows the power of beautiful language to stir and hypnotize, to get to the heart of the matter, but also to confuse the issue, to send the reader dreaming, so she slows her beauty down, roughs it up, breaths air into it, so the reader never dreams through the good parts:

Yes,

And the Voices that come before sleep, that start at the base of my spine.

The doctor is young, handsome almost, says
*they must be the TV or memories of your parents fighting.*

No, I tell him — no,

and what's lovelier than Voices refuting dusk, stippling the world's
ashy assonance.

(from "Asylum")

In the same poem, the reader finds evidence of Bogen's mastery of Whitmanesque verse cataloguing punctuated by rhyme, "That's how you coax something into the box, something bloody or blood-lit,/a headless rooster or snipe — your attention split," and punctuated by rhyme and the article "the," used as a conjunction in the following section *"they ask me to explain the tattoos"*:

The gothic girl the spool of thread the pampered blood the rancid core the two-edged sword the dazzling fire the lazy cur the dying dad the sworn complaint the tinseled tree the buried woe its inky blade the cloak of kin the salty form this book I wrote my slate of skin.

The catalogue is an onslaught of association-as-explanation and urgency that the speaker employs to get at what is at stake as much for herself as for her audience. All through the poems, mythic voices carry on the urgency, warn: "Understanding is best got beyond…." ("Migraine With Aura")

What we have in Deborah Bogen's *Let Me Open You a Swan* is sublime poetry, the rare gift of a terrifying look into the shaping of a warrior poet and her work.

Michelle Mitchell-Foust

## Autopsy: To See For Yourself

In the vault the Master lays the body on the table.
Tenderly he lifts the knife exposing the parts,
touching the body to put a lesson on it, noting
the way the clavicle's fixed with a glue that hardens
like the gum that holds butterfly eggs to a branch.
In the cloister students gather bringing bread
and wine. They have come seeking a lesson.
Amid the sweat and sweetness they work to decipher
the body, to see what is glued together, what floats
in its oily waters. And you are also here, witness
to these rituals, the aligning of descendant with
descendant, cause with cause. Sometimes there's
a flickering in the light that falls on the scene.
Sometimes the whole flock lifts.

# Landscape

*Love is a universal migraine*
*A bright stain on the vision*
*Blotting out reason.*
Robert Graves

*When you awake you will remember*
*everything.*
The Band

## Ghost Images

1/
The mind's a mad cupboard, blackened silver, cups and thimbles.
The mind's a jerky focusing machine still stuck on the girl
who hung by her knees.

And within the camera [opening : closing] — fireworks.
              I mean within the empty box the light's frantic,
grappling with: *the monk, the match, the gasoline.*

The mind is likewise occupied, its light piteously stark, distorted
— but which of us can ever look away?

2/
Into the angular cranium levers lift cold light, but
        how dark and small the box.
And hands must hold the camera still, so stop your breath

        [so stop your breath]

That's how you coax something into the box, something bloody or blood-lit,
a headless rooster or snipe — your attention split.

Seeing the two worlds.

# Asylum

### in admitting

Strange fruits and an early evening moon,

the pleasant rocking with a priest and the scar-faced boy who aped
nonchalance.

They found me too thin, thought my skin shed light, but
I felt as ripe as Marie Antoinette
                      cruising the halls in her ruffled chemise.

When the priest proffered gifts,
a fruit like an orange,
orange-colored, so orange, I saw God's face clearly for a moment —

then the landscape was back. Pristine.
And quaint as a storybook.

### they take a personal history

On the flatbed where they stacked the bales
I stood singing, or

I sat on the splintered bench in Sunday School humming, or

I followed Old John to the mouth of the Missouri where
he yanked slick fishes out.

The grandmother could be fierce.
The grandmother could be kind,
The grandmother said, *Child, be still,*

but a voice rose up in me.

*talk therapy*

Yes.

And the Voices that come before sleep, that start at the base of my spine.
The doctor is young, handsome almost, says
      *they must be the TV or memories of your parents fighting.*

No, I tell him — no,

and what's lovelier than the Voices refuting dusk, stippling the world's
ashy assonance.

And what's more obvious  (I think but do not say)
than God's stuttering:
          broccoli
          brain-on-a-stem
          fat tree alone on a hill.


*dream therapy*

I dreamt a laundromat called Frank N' Sense —
so I knew he'd returned,

but just last week I watched them pitch his ashes into that ravine
behind Mount Wilson.

So how did he make this journey?

      Who taught him to walk in my sleep?

There must be something he's here to say,

something more
I need to give him…

*under hypnosis*

Cigarettes behind Uncle Frank's shed:
endless chores: the stink of hard water:
late night walking to the 2 AM Club: neon said
jazz, said wet juke box low notes: slack-jawed
farm boys: heat on my skin: wood smoke
through drizzle: buttermilk sky: riding home
in a borrowed truck: the catechism of pregnant
women: kettle hot, nail file ready: dreams of dental
tools and small white bones but also Mary's robe:
and a pentagram: and a butterfly pinned to a mat.


*a letter comes from home*

At the end his hand was like that clutch of bones we found
washed up against the pier. Remember? I asked you
how it got there. You mumbled something, then stumbled
but caught yourself just before you toppled.


*they ask me to explain the tattoos*

The gothic girl the spool of thread the pampered blood the rancid core the
two-edged sword the dazzling fire the lazy cur the dying dad the sworn
complaint the tinseled tree the buried woe its inky blade the cloak of kin
the salty form this book I wrote my slate of skin.

*group therapy*

At first I won't.
My arms go slack,
but the clock turns its face to the wall.  I start to write,
I start to write wanting him.
        Wanting them to see his hair slicked back — and the eyebrows.
I want them to remember
        what only I have known.

Him.
Alive at the party.        And torching the shed.

I read that last line out loud, find myself writing faster.
Faster.
Dipping my hands in the ink to find him.


*the guided meditation*

They tell me — see yourself free again,
leaving this island,  this circlet of grey.
At first you won't notice one hand     then the other lifting
stones from the beach.   See yourself doing that, living
outside this circle.
          Alive, you'll feel rocks cutting your feet.
The air may hurt.

You will be leaving the pale fronds feathering the sky,
returning to a noisy forest of other people.

Admit the time's coming when on the boat
      you'll be your own
masthead.
Unable To Turn Back.

*free association therapy*

When will the good girl say her prayers?
      Here are the hairs from out his head.

When will the culprit kiss the glass?
      How does a rattle forget the cough?

This is the sound that drove him mad.
      Why does a fly survive the storm?

How does a wizard earn his keep?
      Show me the stairs that lead to God.


*prognosis*

Late night skaters, the fire gone out, the disappeared moon.

See how the world's gone boney white,
      a blistery storm full of hooks and hammers,
the brain a belfry of memory and shadow —

      and yet we glide, and glide, and glide.

## Using a Blue Willow Pattern, The Anesthesiologist
## Explains the Procedure

See that figure on the bridge? She's on a fierce journey, that girl, pockets
bulging as if she's been stealing apples from an orchard in another world.
It's *elsewhere*, where she's been, not cold or empty so much as a place
where there's a need to be altered — the shadows gathered in — so I must
turn my valves and spigots to make the god-of-the-body lie down.

No one keeps her eyes open with my magic alive in her veins, but it won't
be easy keeping your eyes closed. This sleep's a rough passage so here's
what you should know: *the window through which you will pass becomes a
verandah. You will hear the bird calls of tiny scissors and sense in the yard
elephants shifting their weight.*

## Study Guide

Part of him was tired of holding us,
                  had been gone for weeks,

but another part tried to rise to the occasion
                  kneeling by my bed that morning,
touching my shoulder and talking

        even after he'd purchased the matches.
        And the gasoline.

On the news, I learned he'd brought his Bible with him

        — that he still wore his wedding ring.

The test directions do not recommend leaving
questions unanswered:

Check the box that seems most true.

## Dakota Schism

In Sunday's mirror the red barns
fade, high school girls scrub rouge
from their cheeks, the prize bull apes
a deacon's sneer, crickets choir like
cherubim. Only the grasshopper
carries on, spitting and sawing,
spitting and sawing as the preacher
calls us to *The Upright Life*.

But in our mudrooms lovelorn women
kneel to scrub the dirt-smeared floors
as through the window comes
a sable light Vermeer would love.
In our cellars, votive rhubarb,
on our stairs, a velvet dark.
Therefore, the Aunts dally in the parlor.
Therefore, the Uncles loosen their belts.
We have been another week behind
the reaper. Only God's a pillar.

## Pre-Destination

She needs a man, one who can drive an old Buick right out of
the State, away from old pipes and the stench of sulfur, away from
crickets swaggering across the linoleum and the fog of fish frying
every night. She conjures perfume from the ink coming off movie
magazines, learns to smile through the sting of Old Sunnybrook
going down, then wanders into the pool hall, glowing under low
hanging lights, the room flush with railroad men drinking. She
knows she needs one, a young one hot for the interstate, fat wheel
of winnings stuffed in his jeans and sure as lightning rods bring
down fire, one will come to her. Sure as God's in His Cadillac
Heaven a boy will rise to her occasion. She's restless. Seventeen,
she knows her fate's a Buick that will take her to Montana or
Wyoming. And what's love if not a road map, county line, new
town kind of thing? It's 1945. She falls in love with gasoline.

## Cantilevered Bedtime Story

Wallpaper farm, the girl
with the ducks, the friendly
farmer's father-work,
the moony mother's queer
stare and the bee-hivey
haystacks, the pitchforks,
the curly cows by the pond.

Elsewhere a window frames
green light. Elsewhere,
the dark-hall-doorway,
the long walk to the kitchen's
grown-up talking. The Singer
in the corner, electric
and shiny — and under the bed,
and under the bed…

Happy wallpaper-girl,
the cow wants to give you
her milk. The father's pitchfork
is strong and serene, but what
can be done for the woman
in the fluttering apron
whose gaze is seaward, and
elsewhere, and gone?

## Dakota Grandmother Teachings

The first:
*Have come a long way and arrived tired.* Words on a letter never sent.
Did not say *also pregnant, also to this desolate flatness, the dirt floor,
and fearing wind and fire.* This was her portion of purgatory — sons
who spanned twenty years. A husband who loved his dog.


The second:
*Leave 'em where Jesus flang 'em and turn away* was what she called an
un-Christian sentiment. She didn't believe in looking away. She didn't
want much looking either. She favored the casserole carried warm from
the oven, an expression of Christian fellowship suitable for funerals,
foreclosures and fever among the children.


The third:
Described sweet Jesus hanging dutifully on the you-know-what, lifting
his eyes toward the always-streaming-light of His Heavenly Father who
in some arcane and unintelligible way He also was. This knowledge
might have concerned her had she felt it was her place to understand.
Understanding was best got beyond, she believed.

# Six in the Second Place

means
Horse and wagon part.
Strive for Union. To go on brings
humiliation.

*I Ching*

The girl's hands can't reach
the octave. Her feet dangle above
a carpet that shows a slave market
in ancient Persia, a gorgeous
scene of slaves unloading more
slaves, their skin dark blue

next to the rich red gown of
the Queen. The girl's been playing
the same piece a long time,
her eyes are tired as iron skillets.
On the carpet the auctioneer's
whip cuts a cold apostrophe in

a pale green sky under which
the lapis-colored slaves drag
their brethren to the block.
They want to please the Queen
who sits canopied and bored
beneath the girl's swinging feet.

## Dakota's Omphalos ·

Bare-skinned and beaconish,
sudden,
(like mushrooms)
       silos watch over

Dakota's high plains.

A stringent frugal beauty, ours,
      the attic window's bruisey glow,
a vaulted stillness painted shut,

but there you'll find the shoebox fat with photos,

Granny slim, the girl she'd been aproned,
sky-blown,
            hanging sheets like
sails that can't catch wind.

Spirits here don't let things hold except
these silos, mitered grain.

Long shadows they cast out —
and then at nightfall
reel us in
again.

## Suicide

On July 4th, 1926, my father was born to a woman with red hair and a consumptive husband. A blackbird was clipped to the barbed wire fence outside that woman's window. It flew skyward exposing the red spot under its wing. The question continues. My mind circles it, wary as a bull in a pen.

What was left behind? The consumptive was my dad's first ghost, an inheritance, a grey difficulty, a disordered vision of his father and a bull in a pen, engaged in what my dad thought was a dance.

Here's what I know about my dad: he was a pretty boy buttoned into overalls in 1932. Elementary school and Sunday school and all that teaching about Jesus. He went to war, was coal to the masters, fuel to keep the big trains running. First there was a whistle, then an exercise. There was a specific way to kill a man, which they taught him.

## Special Ed Girl

Remembering meant hoisting into sight,
        but the  teacher said she was too distracted
— said she had a problem with distraction.

People must pay attention to many things at once,
        harmonicas and lemons,
Rush Limbaugh and the different colored paint cans
on the shelves at Home Depot.

But her thoughts were a slow migration,
        this way, they said, feel this.
And she had come to love her own words.

        *Brickle.     Astromi.     Desirening.*

It's unreasonable, they told her, loving what explains
nothing —
but the words lodged themselves in her chest between

the *slickery* heart and the *milkrinous* spine.

## Dakota Migraine

Eye-light cast darkly down
through flat-fingered windmill blades,
       across the barnyard's ruddy cheek –

stark satire of poetry's stare
and the mind's enigmatic architecture.

Conclusions founder here,
       ground to exfoliating bits by

compost,
by roosters
and the shadows of roosters.

# *Religion*

All these died in faith
having never received
the promises.
                        Heb 11: 13-16


*This is not the life I
raised her for.*
                        Edith Boots
                        my grandmother

# Sin

This is the dream: you are the girl,
you are the girl gone now to the
creek, swinging the bucket to and fro,
listening to men who circle the fire.
Mother meant you to go to church,
to wear white gloves and bow your
head. Your body moves on its own,
it flows. It worships fear for you are
the girl, the difficult daughter smeared
with red who ate the fruit they said
would poison — you never listened,
you wouldn't hear, you took the bucket
down to the water, let the cruel cold
cut your feet, this is a dream, you're
deep in the dream, your ankles ache.
You live in the dream of the men
and the dark. You love it here, you
dread the waking.

## Angels

One leg over the motorcycle, I regret the impulse. It's
1969. What we have in common is his brother's suicide
and I know what's running me — enthusiasm, that variant
of fear. The I Ching says enthusiasm in service of the self
is a bad thing. That's the kind of warning I take seriously,
but Roger's dead — and I don't want to start smoking
again. No stars tonight, just dark shapes rising against
darker headlands and part of me aches to be on the bike,
silhouetted against the sky. Soon we're on the slope that
takes us past Olema and Point Reyes, past cryptic horses,
head-down and mellow, stygian banks of nasturtiums and
the rich folks' dogs straining on their chains. The bike's
come wholly to life and the boy directs it. I try to sink into
him so there's no fleshy argument distracting the machine.
The engine's agony drowns out thought as we slide down
to blackness, the sex of wind on our arms and necks. I did
not attend the funeral. I still sing, but not as well as this
bike which tonight is keening. There is something I'm
trying to master. There's no reason to trust the boy whose
bike heads down this mountain.

## Death House Cleared of Belongings

Night doll.  Christmas doll, laying down,
tipping up —
starry eyes disappeared into her head.

Whose eyes loved this strained cold light?
Big God.
Big God who lived in His other country.

Winter's hall. Vast. Cold.  Space unmasking
sad things.

Placeholders.

Wordless hymns stretching me into the far —
into the empty.

Who made me look till I laid down?
I made angels of my own.

# Vocabulary Lesson

*Triangle:*
The sisters had not been equal, but that was nothing to cry about.
At night she lay in bed listening to the sound of the Singer, the
needle humming up and down as mother sewed the matching
outfits. Upon the altar, white lilies and on their feet, black patent
leather shoes. Sometimes there were new words, *bouquet* or
*bolero.* Sometimes they were buttoned into velvet coats and posed
before the house.

*Sickness:*
The book said Lucrezia Borgia slept with her father. In the book,
Lucrezia left town, but eventually the Pope brought her back. The
book said the Pope slept with his daughter, but the natural world
continued to be natural. Babies were born. Children ate their
suppers. Lucrezia became a good cook. When her husband lay ill
she sent a special soup to calm his indigestion.

*Secular:*
She scuffed the toes of her Buster Browns as she walked toward
the library. It was huge — made of stone cut from the Rockies
back when cattle ranchers got so rich they sent their daughters East
for finishing. How dark and cool the Nave. How safe the sanctuary
of the Reference Section where she first discovered pictures of
fallopian tubes blooming like God's own lilies under the plastic
protective cover.

## How at an Early Age I Became Interested in the Mysteries

Somehow I grew large beneath the lamp-light of her
gaze, the plastic doll I bathed each night, her lolling look,
eyes rolling back. I baptized her in the tub, the soapy
water snaking down, and carefully I dried her, bent her
legs to sit her up.

I was good to her, and they to me, my grown-ups with
their rules — good-hearted, yes, but there must be no
crying when the snarls were brushed. Obedience was
everything. For me there was the picking up, the never
(ever) talking back. And for Jesus, they said, his Father's
wish — a cup that would not pass.

Each night they came to claim me, ruffled nightgown
and the brush. They loved to steal the make-believe,
stories from the big black book, me dimming then, light
waning, as they carried me to bed where they stayed to
hear me pray *If I Should Die Before I Wake....*

## Charity

This is the hand stenciled in henna, a hand filled with millet,
millions of grains, and on the fence? That thing's a sparrow or
just some brown bird but let's borrow *sparrow* to name it, for
you are birdless, as I am, your hand topped with millet and
branded in henna, a trap like an ice rink, a trap like a big buffet.

Is there a low lake where no hunters hunker? Are we all under-
handed here in this stillness and what is this hunger, this fervor
for sparrows, for something to touch me, to trust me, to follow
this henna track bird-printed foot path, this food hand? A gift,
I say. A gift, I lie.

## The Book of Changes, Berrigan

The I Ching says it's a problem, Ted. You let your magic tortoise go.
It says: he who knows no limitations will have cause to lament. So I
checked the Book of Lamentations, where *foxes are prowling in Zion*
and *the little ones are gone away as captives* — some days, Ted, I still
think there's way to change their fates.

Today I killed a marmot, read the entrails to see what the gods of
arbitrariness had to offer. They wriggled red in the sun, meaning
I should *Remember the Sweetness of Warblers* one of whom is you,
Ted, but I've never gleaned much comfort from the poetry of grief.
At the library, bums still huddle on the structured steps, turning in
this light to stones. Confucius flew on Ten Wings, Ted, still no one
knows a teaching for *I miss you.* In the shade of the dinosaur my babies
parade waving their innocent flags.

## The Rudest Gesture is the Phone That Rings in the Night

Grant to my brother
that he come here unharmed.
Grant safe passage, that he arrive whole

and please grant to my brother,
        lost now among winds,
        among strange and unknowable winds

a refreshment of breath
that we know the hour of our true meeting,
        the hour of our last parting.

Grant him a moment's ease when the song spinning
in his skull is released,
when his throat softens and opens,

and although I am neither the honey nor the bee,
I ask that you grant me this:
        a dispelling of smoke for my brother
who has been homeward bound
for years.

Grant that he come, penniless or resurrected.
Raise before my face his scarred
and ink-stained palm.

Gently open his mouth once more,
one last time gently open him
that river music
flow.

## This White Bird is Not the Swan

When I was five they
showed me,
said, See the White Bird?

That's the *Anointing*.
        And that man, he's the *one*.
The *one* who foretold the *One*,
        the *one* unfit to tie the *One's*
sandals.

I also could not tie my shoes,
but saw the Mother, the blue robed
Mother.
        There, they said, see her heart,
open and crowned?

Open and crowned, they told me,

and see how her little feet fit on top of the world?

He was a King, her Son.
They said he was a King.

*So did he have had a shiny crown?*

No, child — thorns.

# The Lesson I Taught Myself

He couldn't refuse me, couldn't say *No*,
as I'd said it to the high school boy who loved me,
and later to the young professor.
My legs cinched his ribs as I sang out like
a bronco girl — and later, knees drawn to my chest,
I made a cradle for what I knew would not say
*No*, as God had said it, had said
       *Thou Shalt Not Have*,
sisters withdrawn, fathers blotted out.

There in the night, the cloth that death had spread
on the table turned sanctuary,
       the womb my restitution,
because I could ask,
I could invite fire and make a cauldron of my body
to brew the messy blip on the screen,
the flagrant fish-child never mentioned in the Holy Books.

Thus did I become my own religion.
*Magnified. Rotund.* And when the great Black hovered,
when that Crush Of Cloud was on me, I reveled
in maculate flesh, the great belly a mystery,
the weight of us a warm and bruising power,
       *my own, my other, my more.*

## Poem For My Reader: A Long-dead Sister

Better than sink-work — the poet's desk, the occult
descent into voice,

walking out against the wall of the work.
Keyhole listening.

In Pittsburgh, the dark is never really dark which is the way
I am alone these days

drifting through our unemployed streets,

nothing mine except the whistle of the same train leaving,
box cars empty,

lights of SUVs and townships showing through the slats
and the trains so good at math, at zeros and negative
numbers.

We used to whisper in the big bed
wondering what the grownups were really up to.

Was it sex?

Here's what I know so far: God's long division.

# Transubstantiation

Blood filled floor buckets as the unborn struggled, working her
way into my boney affections. It was Tuesday. My body opened,
swung wide for the doctor with his rubber gloves, his knives, his
occult blood-thirsty education. And that's when I understood Jesus,
when I saw how easy it was to become something else, this vessel,
this portal, this well-oiled gate. I was all those, all feral incarnation
breathing in and out till I fell into a glory of carnival lights, then
back as another breaker forced me to face up to the harsh naked
bulb. That's why I pushed. To stop that. To become myself again.

## Placebo Singers

We rode that long black car to the verdant
astroturf surrounding the sleek dark hole into which
they dropped the body.

No blood.

The blood had been snaked down a drain that
emptied into some septic City culvert.

And during the service, lacing my doubts,
the dark vestibules, the lilies,
       the priests in their sutured robes.

They lifted a cup,
       (an altering thing, a distraction, yes)

praising the vigor of the wine-colored wine.
What clout beauty has —

and how audacious the young priest's promise:
       *He Is Risen.*

They sang their song,
moony vowels as smooth as slinging stones.
They claimed he was
       *At the Very Door of Heaven,*

then priceless in paradox, adept in gesture

they had me step forward to throw dirt
on my Dad.

Note: "Placebo singer" was a medieval term designating parasitic false mourners who attended funerals singing
the "Placebo Domine" to get free food at the reception.

## Sunday, Resurrecting Berrigan

I've named a flower after you, Ted. It's a wild red, back-lit by
yellow and yes, I feel it tango in my jaw and tongue, still it's
hard not to wonder where one goes from here — there's so
much spit and polish on the drunkards, Ted, such a stinking
glow about their heads. Our cherubim squat in squalor and on
the other side of the planet a baby's [BOOM] blown apart, so
why keep at it, and why does your flower, mystical and blood-
laced, stay with me at night?  You'd say it's best to despair,
to keep looking right over the edge of the planet, then you'd
bellow *Cheer Up, nobody's ever known where we go from here*,
but I've always wanted there to be sense to all this, Ted, or
lacking sense, some whimsy. I always wanted to be that girlish
someone waving from the back of a bicycle.

## Six at the Beginning Again

means
Hold to him in truth and
loyalty; This is without blame.

*I Ching*

Love was, I thought, a fire
you set, or failed to set.
Those cold nomadic years,
scouring sand beneath
my feet, I hunted the earthen
bowl, fragile and lovely,

watching Ezekiel's wheel
turn the sky awake. But I
was wrong to think love was
fortune sprung from within,
deservingness stored up so
God could see. It was luck,

all of us fortune-cursed or bit
or blessed. One morning I woke
with the bowl in my hands,
this lover come from where?
*Hold to him in truth and
loyalty. This is without blame.*

## Question

Think of a heart with rooms and nooks, with anterooms and arbors,
a heart blood-red as she rose up to noisy earthly children.
Now think of the white (bone-white) that dressed her hair and narrow
shoulders, and of that gesture — halting, slow, the stare gone ache and hollow.
Her's was a heart of nests and shrines, of molded arch and alley,
architecture born of muscle tried too hard and early.

I walk stark cliffs that front the sea, I take my stand in rock and dirt
and ask you this, on her behalf: how was she meant to house this hurt?

## Resurrection

Reaching back, before you, I find blood rearranged, commingled,
the score re-orchestrated so now there's no me song till cannibal you
began breathing me, sucking me in through the chord, the weight of
you my sumo belly, the harm of you my tooth decay. Child, turning,
you were more than boulders rolling with your hiccups and high jinx,
your mottle and mayhem. You were ticklish and tough, a curvy-
spined angler, so regal, stand-offish, alarming and weird. I feel still
how I harbored the heat of you, the knuckling feet and the beat of the
wild heart, the snare of you fast and fast and fast. You came — your
infantile mission to raise me, untaught and illiterate, sleepy, then not,
ringing the angelus bell in my body. You child, the present. The new
child. The Yew.

# *Migraine*

## Dear My Muse

Your words give me headache
Here, at the temple,
A hurt,
Severing the
Line, and seditiously,
Your tongue      in my head
Which now can't unknow you, not
Now — the tangle of you
Here beneath my skin, a bruisey
Glow.

I'm become your
Host,
You, my mistletoe,
I, with difficulty uprooting myself,
Moving,
You, digging in, and
I now jacklegged and dull.

Grievous one.
You give me a heart-
Aching,
With your gone-grey satchel of purgatory,
        your sow's ear of regret,
And always these colicky visitations —

Some crazy blue moon
              you're here again,
Derelict you,
With your blistery snowstorm, your angling
Hook
And hammer.

## Six at the Beginning

means:
when ribbon grass is pulled up
the sod comes with it.
                    *I Ching*


You know this one, He's old.
And rich. He can do what he
wants. It would even be boring
but there's threat to the soil.
She has the naked glance of
fourteen, hair tucked beneath

her cap and he wants to take
that, the lustrous unveiling.
It's hard to be without the cash
to crush a fat old man, hard to
face it, as you julienne the carrots
in his wife's kitchen. She stands

with a knife in her hands as he
comes downstairs. The curls fall
like ribbons, filling the hollow
at her neck. And though we
want to say at the end that she
recovers wholly, it isn't true.

## Grief is My Addiction

and tonight the ache's a needle in the vein — I mean,

how do I force-feed my heart the voice in my head that says
        you're nothing now, a large hole,

a piece of glassy sky opening, releasing more
nothing.

Fact: you're gone.

But today catching sight of you in the back of another man
I felt that rush —
                    the buzzy heroin of seeing you again.

The shrink calls this "my fiction" but I think it's a simple
dislocation,

like the time I came to in Montreal and wondered —

what is this place?

## *for Pedigree, see Bloodline*


I come back from these outings exhausted.
How can I say it?

On the table, the newspaper.
On the table, his mottled false teeth.

We walk to the pasture to visit his flea-bit mare.
*Here are my keys*, he says.
           He suspects me of enthusiasm.

But once he was the Polestar,
           the Hammer in great Thor's hand.

Once he was large.
The constellation Father.


                    ~


           The Full includes the Void
— the lost and the unlost —

and alcohol's the final fence over which that flea-bit mare
now hangs her head, rolling her eyes
                    as Dad makes people come and go,
                    makes them talk.

And on my hands, these crescent moons,
these pointless stuttering nails tapping and tapping.

Father, answer me this:
           Where does the sound go?

~

Precious reader: Here's a trick I know:

Click, click.    Click. Click. Click.

Are these my nails or his old false teeth?

And would you like to hold them?
You can make folks come and go, teach them
what to say,

but bear with me a moment —
can I get you a drink?

Tell me, friend,
will you be staying long?

## Purgatory

Get up. Recite the names. Twelve people you've never met who were disappeared last night. Now say it: *disappeared,* a word both pristine and charming, but visualize Darkness, and in it a girl, her cut skin exposing muscle that flinches recklessly when doused with salt. Then think of a man on a road, a nail through each palm so he is crucified on asphalt. But you are safe here at home, you are up and online, receiving messages to help you help him. They tell you who to call, who to write. And already you are typing, you are dialing up the senators. You are opening more windows, signing petitions and now you are pledging the radio station and buying an ad in the New York Times. You sit at the table, cutting your heart into little pieces. Everybody's hungry.

## Migraine With Aura

Nota bene:
the derelict house and there in the window
the angry runic angle of my Anglo-Saxon
head.

Alone in this tower I trace arcs
to my temple,
tempering touch to make the Visions disperse
before Revelation claims me.
But for the pain, I would love this blistery
light storm, these castle turrets made
from glassy black and white.

Understanding is best got beyond
some say,
but a one-eyed archer sits at the murder hole,
and already he's taken aim.
God's landscape is obscured by my high-jacked
brain cells, neural pathways wending
to a narrow widow's walk, my head become electric
with suspense: seeing the two worlds.

## Discipline

The older sister explained the technique: sleeping bags strewn on the garage floor, and me, the chosen one, instructed in the art so that it was ceremonial and proper, my breathing deep and measured, deep and deeper, held till I was freighted, lungs hot, hurting, my thumb in my mouth and her arms around me, squeezing.

It was my first complicated and grown-up skill: Trusting. Believing others would be the net, would lay the flesh tenderly down when I left the body behind, conscious-less-ness my achievement, my new and dreamy expertise, and the universe filling with asteroids as I lifted to an embryonic floating and the colored lights of a richer understanding.

It was hard to accept coming back, hard to lose the prehistoric organ music. So hard to drop back into the body with its unruly electric limbs. And how disciplined I was to bear the slow waking, coming to, over me a tent of faces, a rose closing in, that kaleidoscope of girl-stares wanting to know, begging me, *tell us, tell us.*

## Migraine Without Aura

Nota bene:  No stars this time, just
Buddha's knife parting my hair beneath a sky airbrushed
and impotent as my spackled skull and my
stuttering attempts at ignition.

Gone to the void, I'm bared to God's fistic gaze,
a bitch straining her chain as the surgical needle bores through
— but this time, no lights,
the windows of heaven are painted shut.

Alone, I barter, a stake driven down to a vaulted
stillness, to my other,
my stone-
life.

# Threshold

She's bored, lying there — trying
to stay in her body,
like the Special Ed girl reciting the *Pledge of Allegiance*.
There are torn sheets, aluminum lights,
an auctioneer's whip cutting commas in her skin.
She lies fallow
while the white wings circle, while they knit and spin.
The glint is the cutting part of their affections —
the blur, a globe of gas-smother.
She stops her breath a moment, coaxing something
into the box. Lights flicker.

## What Thomas McGrath Taught Me

Dakota
on my skin,
a mark, the family

tattoo,
recessive gene in the pool of our secret
society,

Dakota —
the blotch and blur,
pockmark of my early vaccination,

that smudge and stain and
unmade bed
because Dakota's busy

shoring up an after-hours bar
kept by an unkempt
cousin
as refuge from the psychic
wearies
                    — over there

the hunting shack
                    dogs and rifles.


It's still possible to be alone on the planet.

# Art

We work in the dark.
We do what we can.
Henry James


My angels are losing patience.
Ted Berrigan

## Dream Poem

Jean came,
gave me her
lost book
   — mimeographed pages
folded and stapled.

It doesn't matter, she said.

*It does.*

## About A Girl I Once Was

The country clubs of America looked bleak.
She wanted to peel her stockings off —
        but there was something glinting out
by the 17th hole,
                a silver egg asleep in the sand.

And she desired found objects,

wanted them to split her tongue, to cleave minnows
from water, sequins from satin.

Her party toenails glistened. Her back
sleeked down to her hips and she swore she could feel
something swannish in that egg.

So what should I have told her?
That night is just a painted backdrop?

In that dark she felt a great nothing —
                heard only the Voice saying

*do not try to cover yourself.*
*Do not drop the egg.*
*Soon it will begin to hum.*

## Working to Decipher the Body

*Albers' Homage to the Square:*

He didn't want to elevate it, just make you see the shimmer edging a square that presents precision to effect emanation. He wanted to get it talking — and you, he wanted to change you too, meant to force that retinal shiver in response to green on gray, gray on yellow.

If you take a walk in the forest, pick up a leaf and hold it to the light.

*Diebenkorn's Knife:*

There's power in naming — the inconsequential suddenly centered. The table upon which the knife reclines is now more *table*, and above it the quadrilateral blue becomes *window*. You must stop your breath. Soon *couches* and *chairs* emerge.

*Matisse's Blue Cut Outs:*

They argue for evolution. What might be a third leg is likely a tail. Something is being passed from hand to hand. Even more confusing then, the apples and a figure we can't quite recognize.  Human?

*Picasso's Woman with Book:*

In moments of intellectual work or trancey reverie it remains critical that the nipples are accessible.

## Young Swan

The teenage girl has a heart like a toaster oven.
It doesn't help that she's always hearing
the drunks on the corner say: *That one, she's
a little heart breaker.*

Her mother doesn't like the way she wears
her fuschia lipstick — she keeps threatening to
cancel the tooth-whitening sessions but
the girl with the toaster oven heart comes to my
after-school art class wearing that pink
to light her slick white teeth.

I have a heart like a TV. Someone out there's
always pressing the remote. The girl with
the blinding teeth has artificial hair,
but it's not right to say it's not really her hair.
She saved up to have it crimped and curled
at the corner shop.  And me, I'm an old bird
— too old to be surprised.
All swans busk to claim their territory.

## Dear Berrigan, You Died

Now how will we know if we've stored sufficient nectar?
Letters, birds, beggars, books — but where's the poem to keep
me from reaching into the darkened cookie jar, to stop the
descent into my sadder Stygian self? Ted, there are still
mysteries I need to master: why that semblance of tenderness
in the hands of the sociopath who is not angry as she holds
her children under? And why does most love wait to grow its
shape till the names are inscribed, so it's just stone crying out
to the one not here? I'm a hand writing these lines, Ted, a
girlish enthusiasm pursuing you into the earth. Oh my dear
Berrigan, you died.

## The Migraine's Art

Blackwork —
this wanting to unravel, to travel lonely at the edge of  the road
yoked to an undiscovered purpose, wintry
and so far gone
this me, this mist, this ashy unraveling chained
to the axe in my crown

                        harried by heaven's hurt
and craving a beggar's bed
        for the fox is out and bells are tolling fire
or priests,
        their knuckles a nick in my skull.

## Concerning Failure

Blood on the gateposts, proclamations from the speakers,
grimy manifestos nailed to factory doors.
Alive and salivating we left the graduation early,
made for Berkeley or Mendocino seeking the boney wings
of revolution.

We wanted Free Clinics, Free Parks and Free Food Banks.
Daycare, short work weeks and *Grace*.
We wanted the Harmonies of the Heavens to manifest

and we had Che's glamorous grin, Black fists raised
like lamp posts — we had town meetings and our righteous indignation,
but we became the bodies dragged and beaten by irate
batons deployed to save the rich from kids who could see
the two worlds,

tenderhearted kids, stoned on the cigarettes of brotherhood
and revolution — children making angels of their own.

## Injured Swan

The nights I sleep best I dream about being
shot. Not getting shot.
I'm already shot.
The dream's flimsy. I'm silky. The hole in my shoulder
goes straight through, but there's no blood —
       I barely bleed at all.

Undress slowly, he said, and in the dream
I did that. Then he did something, then I did too but
there was a hole in that doing.
a soft weeping wound in it, and a comma
before the kissing commenced.

Sometimes there's a gun. Sometimes not, but the dress
is always filmy, my shoulders always bare.
In dreams, they say, your heart will tell,
so sometimes I wonder,
       maybe this dream is a wish my heart fakes
sleeping deeply, wearing the billowy dress
— for I dream often of being shot, but
I barely bleed at all.

# The Artist's Statement

*All these died in faith without
having received the promises.*
Heb 11: 13-16

When Jay De Feo finished *The Rose*, her problem was how to preserve
it. It had to be sealed up and stored away so that after she died they could
re-discover it, haul it up from the Whitney's basement and celebrate it.

If I could unearth Jay De Feo I'd tell her she's famous now but maybe
it's time to stop bothering the dead, time to stop wondering if they miss
the sex of wind on their arms, or whether they're like Olema's dogs,
chained and howling into a gaping dark. Maybe they *are* a gaping dark
but in the end even de Feo had to stop trying to master it all. She had to
count her remaining teeth and try to preserve the work.

## Words I Had To Teach My Spellcheck

*for Jerilyn Sillers*

First of all *spellcheck*, which it wants to separate
into two small — two separate — words
for wrong,

then *suckiest* without which I cannot talk about Lynn's
surgery or the war,

and since I've never learned to live with the fact
that when I'm not thinking about you
probably nobody is,

I have forced it to remember the spelling of your name
which is not unique, simply nearly-so,

and *nearly-so*, which I guess is not a word at all

but so *a propos* these days when the spellcheck rejects
*oomph*, claiming I must mean
                *voodoo*
                or *booboo*
                or *love, mom*.

## The Human Condition

Evil-eyed is a verb in Greek.

Master builders are born, but their lives are too short for their own designs.

We're bodies of water in biology but not in geography,

and even in the closet of our lesser selves we're drawn to a light coming under the door.

Within each ear                    a small screw squeaks.

Woodpeckers come to our windows in hunger.

## Forgiveness Poem

Broken memory — failing light, each pearly thought
a window filmed with soot,
but I think he meant to hold us, meant to rise
to the occasion
                    and if his head ached,
if light's scissors were relentless,
if his eyes turned anthracite,
alive with a clean flame until he saw only that which
unhinged him,
if, for him, there was no easing into nightfall
          — just the shadow of a silo reeling him in,
then understanding is best got beyond.
I believe.

## Fire, and the Sewing of Sky

In the catholic glow of the snow I set out
dreaming of heat
            and the forget of sorrow.

Sadly some, but not all
and onward I desire to wake, to weave my heat with snow.

For color, blue.  For spill,
water.
For sunrise — fire, and the sewing of sky.

It's winter's muted path I wander,
I, who have always loved the bedlam of thunder and church bells unkempt
                and far-flung in their steeples.

Today I choose yellow,
                a yolk in the pan.
A yolk in the sky.

Some say it's a snare,
            that always the thief mistakes his master,

but why bristle and strain after shadows
which are really shut lamps?

Let the lost ones go —
let the bell of your questioning shudder and still.

Unclench your heart.

Let me open you a swan.

## To See For Yourself

You'll need a bone saw and a skull chisel,
a scalpel and scissors. You'll need
toothed forceps, a basin of water —
you'll need time. But even with the tools,
even with a silvery light flickering on all that
metal, it will be difficult to detach
the eggs from the branches, the fiery dreams
from your sleep.

It's love that knuckles down, that struggles
to tell the tumor from the bright idea,
paring memory to bone and turning truth into
something better than monument.
There will be months and years when you can't
see, a gauzy past in the air and no light.
Then one day, the flock lifts.

# Notes

It's hard to describe my debt to Ted Berrigan's constructive artistry. It is with humility and gratitude that I try in this book to continue his line-swapping tradition by using a few Berrigan lines in the three poems that speak to and about Ted. I hope you will be inspired to read (again) his wonderful Sonnets.

1. *The Book of Changes, Berrigan* uses versions of two lines from Ted Berrigan's Sonnets:
> "Bums huddle on the structured steps, turning in this light to stones", and
> "My babies parade waving their innocent flags."

2. *Sunday, Resurrecting Berrigan* uses versions of three lines from Ted Berrigan's Sonnets:
> " Where does one go from here?", "Go down over the side of the planet", and
> "...that girlish someone waving from the back of a bicycle."

3. *Dear Berrigan, You Died* uses versions of two lines from Ted Berrigan's Sonnets:
> " Dear Berrigan He Died" and "a hand is writing these lines."

## Poetry Titles from Elixir Press

*Circassian Girl*
by Michelle Mitchell-Foust

*Imago Mundi*
by Michelle Mitchell-Foust

*Distance From Birth* by Tracy Philpot

*Original White Animals* by Tracy Philpot

*Flow Blue* by Sarah Kennedy

*A Witch's Dictionary* by Sarah Kennedy

*Monster Zero* by Jay Snodgrass

*Drag* by Duriel E. Harris

*Running the Voodoo Down*
by Jim McGarrah

*Assignation at Vanishing Point*
by Jane Satterfield

*The Jewish Fake Book*
by Sima Rabinowitz

*Recital* by Samn Stockwell

*Murder Ballads* by Jake Adam York

*Floating Girl (Angel of War)*
by Robert Randolph

*Puritan Spectacle* by Robert Strong

*Keeping the Tigers Behind Us*
by Glenn J. Freeman

*Bonneville* by Jenny Mueller

*Cities of Flesh and the Dead*
by Diann Blakely

*The Halo Rule* by Teresa Leo

*Perpetual Care* by Katie Cappello

*Prelude to Air from Water*
by Sandy Florian

*Let Me Open You A Swan*
by Deborah Bogen

## Fiction titles

*How Things Break* by Kerala Goodkin

*Nine Ten Again* by Phil Condon

## Limited Edition Chapbooks

*Juju* by Judy Moffat

*Grass* by Sean Aden Lovelace

*X-testaments* by Karen Zealand

*Rapture* by Sarah Kennedy

*Green Ink Wings* by Sherre Myers

*Orange Reminds You Of Listening*
by Kristin Abraham

*In What I Have Done & What I Have Failed To Do* by Joseph P. Wood

*Hymn of Ash* by George Looney

*Bray* by Paul Gibbons